the GOD BOX

Sharing my mother's gift of
faith, love and letting go

MARY LOU QUINLAN

WORTHY
PUBLISHING

Published by Worthy Publishing, a division of Worthy Media, Inc.,
134 Franklin Road, Suite 200, Brentwood, Tennessee 37027.

HELPING PEOPLE EXPERIENCE THE HEART OF GOD

eBook available at www.worthypublishing.com

Library of Congress Control Number: 2012953025

The author acknowledges that when presented in the main body copy of the
book, text from certain handwritten notes was edited for readability.

For foreign and subsidiary rights, contact Riggins International Rights
Services, Inc., www.rigginsrights.com.

ISBN: 978-1-617951-82-4 (hardcover w/ jacket)

Design and composition by Rachel Cost and Greenleaf Book Group LLC
Creative direction by Lissa Lowe
Photography by Mark Laita
Illustrations by Kathryn Whyte

Printed in the United States of America

13 14 15 16 17 LBM 11 10 9 8 7 6 5

Dedicated to Mom and Dad
Always together, even in Heaven

contents

introduction

L ast fall, I wrote an essay about a discovery my family made after losing my mom. We found her God Box, in which she had stowed dozens of tiny handwritten messages to God on our behalf. My father, brother and I always knew Mom loved us and knew that she placed petitions for us in her God Box, but it wasn't until we found this treasure that we truly realized just how deeply and unselfishly she cared for so many years.

The groundswell of feedback in response to that essay took me by surprise. I heard from women who missed the mothers they had lost, as well as from those lucky enough to still be close with their moms. Some wrote that, despite being distant from their own parents, they had started the God Box tradition so that someday their own children would know how loved they were.

"Ever my
guardian angel,
MY MOM WOULD CONTINUE TO TEACH ME
ABOUT MYSELF, EVEN AFTER HER DEATH."

Their letters caused me to dig deeper into my mom's God Box. The more I reread what she had written, the more I realized that these notes filled with loving words were more than mementos. Fingering each slip of paper, I could reclaim her sparkle and common sense, her humor and optimism, and–above all–her enduring spirit. And ever my guardian angel, Mom would continue to teach me about myself, even after her death.

Since her passing, pieces of her personality and spirit have become part of me. Her influence showed gradually at first–a change of heart, a gesture of kindness–until at last I came to understand that her greatest gift wasn't inside the God Box, but in the lessons she taught me that transformed my life for good.

Shortly before my father died, I told him I was writing Mom's story for publication. Dad clapped his hands together and grinned from ear to ear. "Your mother would be so thrilled!" he said. He knew her so intimately that his permission was akin to getting hers. And as her daughter and confidante, I was careful to guard what I knew she would want kept secret and sacred.

Yet sometimes we never know our parents' inner

thoughts until it's too late. Despite our closeness, when Mom passed away, I still wished I knew more of what she held in her heart. By reading the contents of the box, I would come to understand the unspoken pain and fear she shielded from us, the daily depth of her devotion to our family, the breadth of her empathy. The God Box would turn out to be our favorite heirloom, handmade by Mom herself. The slips of paper told the story of what mattered most to her, all in her signature candor and soulful voice.

But if I thought I had heard all I could from my mom by reading each note, I was wrong. A few weeks ago, rummaging around in an old jewelry box of mine, I found a piece of torn paper with this message, dated exactly twenty years before.

"I love you. You will always be in my God Box."

This book is my way of sharing her gift of faith, love and letting go.

Mary

My mother's name was Mary. I am her namesake and her soul mate.

I lost her on May 29, 2006, as the Memorial Day fireworks kissed the sky good night. It was just Mom and me. I believe she planned it that way. Though she lay in a coma from a terrible stroke, I still felt I could read her mind.

I knew she couldn't bear to look one last time into the eyes of her beloved husband–my father, Ray–or hug my brother, Jack, good-bye. But me? She knew I could take it. I was her best friend.

When she breathed her last breath, her hand in mine, I swear I could feel her spirit lift into that firecracking sky. She took a part of me with her.

* * *

"I WAS DADDY'S GIRL BUT
my mother's
daughter."

I was Daddy's girl but my mother's daughter. I never had any children of my own so I was never the mother. Instead, I spent my life trying to get an A, even an A+, in daughter. I know that not everyone loves their mother this way, but I did, and there's nothing I wouldn't give to hear Mom's full-throated laugh again or to feel her hug that squeezed right through the phone to me.

Perhaps it's inevitable that we become our mothers, but I was my mother from the start. We both loved sexy shoes and scary movies. We both worked in advertising, disliked braggarts and beat ourselves up if we hurt anyone's feelings. My hips are uneven, just like hers, but unfortunately, she gave her beautiful curly red hair to Jack instead of me. (From time to time, I've colored some red into my hair because it makes me feel closer to her.)

9

Mom and I had secret names for each other. I called her "Mare," short for Mary, just to be fresh, or "Marmie," the name of the kind mother in *Little Women*. She called me "Anna Banana." I never knew why.

We shared bad habits too. She taught me how to eavesdrop. If, when we were out for one of our girls-only lunches she'd spot upset faces on the couple in the booth behind me, she'd say under her breath, "Don't look!" We'd pretend to eat our salads while we rolled our eyes at an overheard break-up.

We both were magnets for people who wanted to divulge their deepest secrets. (And, thanks to our amazing intuitive powers, we assumed we knew what they were going to say next. We were wrong more often than not, but that didn't stop us from finishing other people's sentences, a quirk of mine that my patient husband, Joe, finds particularly exasperating.)

> "We both were magnets for people WHO WANTED TO DIVULGE THEIR DEEPEST SECRETS."

For years, Mom and I shared a code for our closeness: "Hands on." We ended every nightly phone call by pressing our palms to our receivers and saying "Hands on," which meant that we were always together, even when living far apart. She had retired to Florida with Dad twenty years before her death, and whenever I left her at the airport, I would drop my luggage on the curb and press my hand to her car window. She would place her palm on the inside glass, her fingers lined up against mine, and we'd both mouth the words "Hands on."

I whispered it to her that last sad night we had together.

* * *

I miss so much about Mom, especially the way she could make me feel that everything would be okay. She could solve any situation, from a scraped knee to a broken heart, with a prayer. She prayed for every need, hurt or hiccup that hit Dad, Jack and me, and our spouses and kids, as well as friends and neighbors. Mom was so naturally empathetic that even strangers poured out their troubles to her. She always promised to keep everyone in her prayers, no matter what their religion or beliefs.

She inhaled a worry. She exhaled a prayer. Truth be told, Mom was holier than the rest of our family, but she wasn't a holy roller, if you know what I mean. Deep inside, she just believed. During our family's early years in Philadelphia, Mom relied on a pretty standard Catholic repertoire of novenas and rosaries and Mass for whatever ailed Dad or Jack or me. Every once in a while she would call the Sisters of St. Joseph to ask them to put in a good

11

"She could solve anything,

FROM A SCRAPED KNEE TO

A BROKEN HEART,

WITH A PRAYER."

word Upstairs if one of us was sick or a big exam was coming up.

But by the time Mom and Dad had settled in Florida in the mid-'80s, there was more to ask for. Jack and I had grown up and started families of our own. I married Joe Quinlan and moved to New York City. Jack and his wife, Sandy, had two little girls, Kelley and Meghan. We had busy, challenging careers and lives up north, and Mom was separated from us by so many miles. The passing years brought new health problems for both of my parents. And, once Mom had more free time in Florida, her empathetic nature attracted an ever-expanding list of people who adopted her as their personal counselor as soon as they met her. Their concerns became hers.

Mom needed a better way to cope with the growing list of worries weighing on her shoulders and her mind. That's when the God Box was born. She started writing down her petitions on random scraps of paper that she addressed to God and then placed into her God Box for resolution and relief.

Whenever we had a hope or a concern, Mom would cheerfully offer, "I'll put it in the God Box." Just hearing that made me feel like my issue of the moment was somehow worthy. If it was important to me, it was important to Mom. And if it was important to Mom, into the God Box it went.

It wasn't odd that Mom took to this very simple solution. She was a fixer and a doer with a practical bent. She was an early adopter of convenience foods, instant messaging, and automatic bill paying. The God Box was an easy way to make good on her promises to help.

*   *   *

On the night before her funeral, Dad, Jack and I felt like dishrags. Dad kept shuffling from room to room. He couldn't even look at Mom's recliner, so still next to his. Jack pretended to care about the work on his laptop. I threw myself into every detail of preparing the service because "doing" is what I do best.

My Mom, ever the planner, had left behind hints of what she wanted for her service. In her desk drawer, for instance, I found the programs from her friends' memorial services, and she had checked off the hymns she liked. On one pamphlet, she had marked "good choice!" next to "Spanish Eyes," but I nixed that in favor of "Ave Maria."

I had already written Mom's eulogy and had read it to

"None of us felt as shiny
WITHOUT HER IN THE ROOM."

her while she lay in a hospice room. It's not that I wanted to jinx her. I just wanted her to hear how much we loved her. When I gave it to Jack to review, his eyes filled with tears. "How am I going to read this out loud? I can't even read it to myself without crying."

If Mom had been there, she would have teased us into cheering up because she was such an effervescent, fun woman. She was always up for a good time, turning up the volume if Willie Nelson was on the radio, dressing up her khakis with a bangle belt just to go out for breakfast. Even at eighty-two, Mom was the life of our party. None of us felt as shiny without her in the room.

We were each picking at our takeout dinner on the back porch when Jack asked, "Where's Mom's God Box?" The three of us looked at each other, forks in midair. For all the times she had mentioned it, Mom had never told us where she kept her little cache of prayers.

17

discovery

The God Box was Mom's secret stash of notes to God. She'd grab any handy piece of paper–from a "While you were out" slip to a receipt or a Post-it note–and scribble, "Dear God, Please take care of . . ." She would dash off a petition in her natural, heartfelt style, date it and sign it "Love, Mary." Then she would keep folding the paper until it was really small and place it safely in the box.

The God Box came with one caveat. If any of us ever re-worried about the request, Mom would say, "If you think you can handle it better than God, it's coming out." Just the suggestion that we thought we were more powerful than God put us in our places and made us stop fretting and start believing. I don't think Mom ever made good on her threat, but her advice encouraged us to try to let go.

We loved how the God Box gave her such comfort and relief, and we were always happy to have our hopes and fears stored inside. However, no one believed in its power as deeply as Mom did.

* * *

On the night before Mom's funeral, I headed back to my parents' bedroom to search for the God Box. It was the first time I had gone in there since Mom died. I felt as if she might walk in at any second; I could even smell her fragrance. Everything was still in its place: There were the flowered bedspread and the matching curtains we had hung together. And there was the family gallery she had created, photos of each of us on the wall, the bureau and her nightstand.

I looked in her dresser where slips and nightgowns waited, unneeded. No box. Her closet was crowded with pastel skirts and floral dresses and palm tree purses, reminders of lunches together and parties gone by. I found the white leather jacket (a duplicate of mine) I had bought her for her eightieth birthday. But still no box.

I was about to give up when I glanced up to the highest

shelf. Mom would have had to stand on her tiptoes to shove anything up there. I ran my hand along the edge and brushed against something rough. I pulled down a small round wicker box. I flipped open the lid and inside I could see pieces of paper covered with Mom's handwriting. "I found it!" I yelled. Then I paused. On a hunch, I reached up to the shelf again, stretching to feel further back. My hand hit another box. I grabbed a chair to stand on and found another box and another and another– wood, ceramic, glass, cardboard.

My arms filled with mismatched containers, I walked back to the dining room table and set seven God Boxes down gently in front of Dad and Jack. Dumbfounded, we each chose one and opened the lid. Every one of them was stuffed tight with tiny wedges of paper, folded over and over like origami.

We turned the boxes upside down and hundreds of notes tumbled out. We started unfolding and reading, shouting out the dates: "2003!" "1994!" "1989!" We were stunned. We were face-to-face with every molehill and mountain of our family's life dating back twenty years.

21

Every wish and hope and worry, every decision small or big, everything Mom ever prayed for lay before us in a pile of scraps written in her hand.

Mom had left behind a diary of our family's life, her love letter to us in a thousand pieces.

* * *

Mom's notes weren't requests for world peace. She asked for help with the trials of everyday life, like this petition: "Dear God, Please make my right ankle stop hurting. Love, Mary." There were mentions of so many things we had forgotten, like office spats or real estate quandaries. We weren't the only ones in the box: we found messages about our extended family, about people we'd never met, about people who leaned on Mom for answers and hope.

The first paper was dated August 7, 1986. Though nearly all of the notes were scrawled hurriedly in Mom's hand, this one was typewritten, with perfect margins and indentations. She had typed it on the back of a sheet of office stationery–a souvenir from her last job as a secretary in an advertising agency. Maybe Mom wanted her first letter to God to look official. She summed up everything that was on her mind.

August 7, 1986

Dear Lord:

Protect my good health --
my eyes -- my family - my dear
husband.

Protect Jack in decisions
in his job. Protect Marylou and
Joe in their jobs, and especially
a decision on buying this house in
New Hope.
Thank you for all of our
blessings. You are with us always.
Love   Mary

"Mom had left behind a
diary of
our family's life,
HER LOVE LETTER TO US IN A THOUSAND PIECES."

I love that message because it shows how Mom wrote to God like a pen pal would, so straightforward and friendly. Her mind ricocheted from one thought to another, as mine still does.

I'm not sure why Mom mentioned her eyes, unless that was around the time when the optometrist found a suspicious iris freckle. I remember that scared her. I have one too–something else we shared.

"We loved how the God Box gave her such comfort
AND RELIEF, AND WE WERE ALWAYS HAPPY
TO HAVE OUR HOPES AND FEARS STORED INSIDE."

24

But Mom was right to question the wisdom of our buying a tiny farmhouse in Bucks County, Pennsylvania. As relative newlyweds and apartment dwellers, my husband, Joe, and I were clueless about old houses and could barely make the down payment. But we put in a bid, on the spot, because we were instantly charmed by the 140-year-old house despite its single bathroom and sketchy septic system.

The house turned out to be a godsend for our family. We invited my parents to live there with us every summer after they moved to Florida to get out of the heat, which gives you a sense of just how generous and mellow Joe is. Mom and Dad, never wanting to overstay their son-in-law's kind invitation, would insist on sleeping outside in their RV when we had overnight guests. I always felt embarrassed when our friends noticed the lights in the motor home parked in the driveway. "Oh, that's my parents. They don't want to interfere."

Most of the time, however, they stayed in the bedroom next to ours. When I returned to our Bucks County home after the funeral, I found three more God Boxes that Mom had stashed there, each full of notes about our summers together.

Ten God Boxes in all–a testament to Mom's commitment to her ritual.

* * *

Every summer during their visit, Mom and Dad would borrow our car, and one night they hit a deer on their way home from dinner. They were distressed that our car's fender had been smashed into the front tire, but Mom was even more upset when a stranger drove up to the accident scene and loaded the dead creature into his trunk. She felt worse when the insurance company refused to cover the back fender scraped by an aggressive tow truck driver. Mom turned to divine intervention, I discovered: "Dear God, Please take care of insurance for the Mazda. Let them know it was caused by towing. Love, Mary." (I guess God was supposed to call up State Farm and work it out.) The truth was Joe and I could handle the expense, yet Mom must have spent weeks feeling guilty. I wish she hadn't.

Another slip written during a summer sojourn read, "Please let the Pergo floor be the right choice." Dad was doing me a favor by converting a garage into an office. He and I had chosen the pale oak grain together, so she needn't have been concerned I wouldn't like it. But because the house was mine, she wanted it to be perfect for me. All I wanted was for it to be perfect for her.

That was the nature of our mutual admiration. Sometimes during our conversations I would suddenly say "More!" which meant, "I love you more!" Then Mom would say "More!" and then I would, and we'd go faster and faster, laughing and riding over each other—"more,

"Mom wrote to God like a pen pal would,

SO STRAIGHTFORWARD AND FRIENDLY."

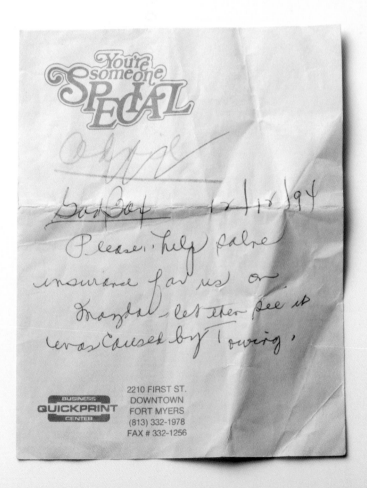

"FINDING THE GOD BOXES WAS like reading Mom's heart."

more, more"–until one of us gave up. It was never me.

*   *   *

Finding the God Boxes was like reading Mom's heart. It was incredible to see the sheer scope of her faith, so certain, so unedited. Her unconditional belief in God came alive for me, as fresh as I remembered it from all the years of growing up as her daughter and best friend. Opening the little letters was like feeling her hug all over again.

I began reading and, box by box, year by year, walked backward through my life.

29

faith

Whenever I leaf through my mother's petitions, I am taken back to childhood nights when she first taught me how to pray. When I was just four or five, she would urge me to get down on my little pajama-clad knees, fold my hands and rattle off the list of names she had helped me memorize.

"Dear God, Please watch over Mommy and Daddy, Jack and me . . ." and then I would move on to my grandparents, alive and gone. A hearty "Amen!" and I would climb into bed. Mom would stay for a few minutes, her hand softly stroking my eyes shut until I fell asleep.

Surely she prayed for me as I dozed off under her palm. I felt so safe with her. Believing in God was easy with Mom at my side.

"Reading through Mom's God Box,

I UNDERSTOOD JUST
HOW FULLY
SHE BELIEVED."

* * *

I grew up proud to be Mom's good girl. Jack was the boy version. We both excelled not only in subjects like arithmetic and spelling but also in our Catholic school's moral Olympics: obedience, cooperation, self-control, courage, perseverance, cleanliness and health habits.

Each Sunday at church, I lined up with all the other little girls, wearing my lacy chapel veil or, in a pinch, a Kleenex fastened to my curls with a bobby pin. With the nuns over my shoulder and Mom as my coach, my spiritual life got off to a promising start.

My prayer list continued to grow over time to include more relatives and friends until my freshman year of high school, when I added my final name–Bobby Kennedy. I graduated from high school and then college and gradually lost my religious rhythm. After marrying and moving to New York–"Sin City" to a Philly girl–my formal practice became somewhat à la carte. I was running from meetings to airports, building a career, a new marriage and new friendships. Getting to church every week seemed to slide off my to-do list.

But some habits die hard. I still make a surreptitious

sign of the cross for the victim when an ambulance races by. I always pray a silent "Hail Mary" when my plane takes off, and I send good vibes to the universe when we close yoga class with "Namaste." But using the excuse of a busy life, I downshifted my conversations with God to asking for favors on the run, like, "Please let me ace this job interview today." I became expert at pitching heavenly bargains: "If this mammogram is good, I swear I'll go to Mass more often."

Clearly my erratic style paled in comparison to my mother's steady practice of unshakable faith.

* * *

And practice she did. Jack and I talked to Mom nearly every day no matter where we traveled or how late the hour. We would spill the silly and serious minutia of our days from hurt feelings to missed flights onto her willing shoulders. Mom listened to every detail of our lives and made it her business to try to make everything better. She'd hand out advice or sympathy, congratulations or caution. While we chatted, I could picture her at her kitchen counter, penning notes on the back of a shopping list for later insertion in the box.

But no matter the date or the sentiment, there was a recurring theme in the God Box that was vintage Mom. And that was her vigilance about our churchgoing habits.

Mom used to notice that I was slacking off on my Sunday routine, even though I tried to hide it during the summer by leaving occasional church programs lying around as proof of my attendance. I thought I had Mom convinced. But in the God Box, the embarrassing truth came out.

"Please let Mary Lou go back to church and visit. And return Joe to the faith." I thought it was funny that Mom blamed Joe for my absenteeism. He is as Catholic as I am. But Mom would never blame me for anything.

Mom wrote a lot of notes hoping that Jack would return to church after he'd married Sandy, who was a "public," as we used to call the non-Catholics when we were kids. Mom adored Sandy and never tried to convert her, but I think that while babysitting her granddaughters Kelley and Meghan, Mom may have performed a citizen's baptism by throwing water on them. Mom often campaigned in the God Box that the girls enroll in parochial school, but that was never going to happen.

To compensate for our behavior, Mom would cover for us in the God Box. When she would ask for a favor for us, she'd sign off with a defense of our loyalty: "Mary Lou loves you" or "Jack is coming back soon!"

* * *

While the God Box was Mom's go-to problem solver, she also relied on more traditional talismans. Whenever I flew home after a Florida visit, I'd later find that she had sneaked a saint's medal into my briefcase. I can imagine her grinning as she did it. Mom was always on me to keep the faith.

She herself never missed Sunday Mass unless she was really under the weather. She loved holding Dad's hand during services, even when he nodded off during long sermons (or, as he would protest, "meditated") while sitting with his hands on his knees, palms upturned and eyes closed in a yogi-like trance.

But Mom's faith wasn't blind. In the God Box, she scolded the priests who thought they were entertainers. If their jokes had been funny, I know Mom would have laughed along, but corny one-liners really ticked her off. As a rule, I think Mom preferred nuns since they were just as hardworking as she was.

Mom also frowned on the soloists who expected applause after every hymn. "This isn't a show, you know," she would grumble. She believed

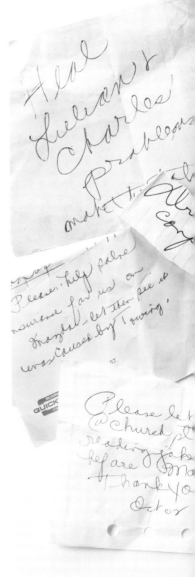

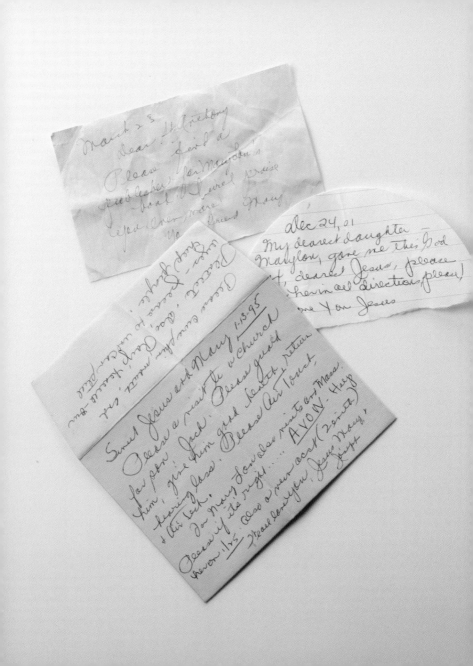

their songs were prayers, not opening numbers. So, when the crowd erupted in mandatory ovations, our usually sunny family would sit, stone-faced, with our hands stubbornly clasped in our laps to show our support for Mom's anti-Vegas position.

* * *

Mom was unabashedly committed to God and entrusted her most intimate wishes to the sanctity of the God Box. When friends and relatives called her with their problems, she would tell them, "You're in my God Box," as a way to ease their concerns. I loved that she was able to give and receive such solace from these humble containers. Once, when she had brought out her box and I saw how dog-eared it had become, I bought her a new one made of stained glass. Mom displayed it on her coffee table instead because it was too fancy to suit the job. To her, the God Box was supposed to be simple, just like the gesture of surrendering her cares.

But even Mom admitted that letting go was hard. Inside her hand-typed autobiography, with its cover illustration of yellow daisies and its giveaway title "Mary's Beautiful Memories," Mom confessed that when she initiated the ritual, she struggled to forget about her stowed-away

39

cares. "At first, it was hard," she wrote. "I had to practice putting them in and letting them go."

As I read the collective years' worth of entries, I noticed that sometimes she would ask for the same request multiple times. I attributed that to her unflagging ability to hope, not to any doubt that she hadn't been heard.

* * *

Reading through Mom's God Box, I understood just how fully she believed. And I realized that I hadn't lost my own faith; I had just channeled my prayers through her. I knew she was representing me to God while I was busy believing I could fix anything by focusing my energy and working hard, another lesson Mom had taught me. "One foot in front of the other," she would say.

40

But reading between the lines, I sensed that I had missed out on something that fueled and sustained my mother. Even when she was missing us or scared, she had a partner through all her trials.

I used to have Mom. When she died, I was left on my own. Could I learn again to ask for help from a higher power, as my mother had taught me?

love

Diaries are personal by nature, and the God Box was no exception. My mother's notations were as honest and openhearted as she was. And just as diaries often disclose the identity of a true love, the God Box revealed the man at the center of Mom's universe–her husband, Ray Finlayson. I never doubted that Mom was head over heels in love with Dad, but the contents of the notes confirmed they were as devoted in their golden years as when they first met in 1945.

Inside the God Box, for example, I found a tiny scrap that wasn't a letter or a request. It held these words: "Always together, even in Heaven." Early in their marriage, Mom and Dad adopted that phrase as their lifetime mantra as a couple. Dad engraved the words on a gold pendant that my mom wore for as long as I can remember.

* * *

Dad fell in love with Mom when he dropped into a USO dance while on leave in Philadelphia near the end of World War II. Trim and tall in his tan army uniform, Dad was instantly drawn to the vivacious twenty-one-year-old redhead who was volunteering as a hostess. One minute she was giggling with her girlfriends, the next she was dancing in his arms.

The USO had a rule for the hostesses: "Never accept a ride home with a serviceman on the first night!" But Mom sensed something special about the dark-haired soldier and accepted his offer of a lift. Weeks later, when my grandmother met Dad, she looked him over and said, "I'm so glad that Mary has fallen for an older man." He was twenty-seven.

* * *

They were married on June 11, 1949. Dad said it was the happiest day of his life. After paying for the reception, the flowers, and a weekend in the Poconos, my parents started their life together with the $12 that were left in their Corn Exchange bank account. Four years later I was born, and then Jack, the little redhead, came in 1954. We all lived in

43

a small row house in north Philadelphia where hard work was expected and the love was guaranteed.

Our parents were crazy about us, but Jack and I both recall a serious conversation during which they told us that as much as they loved us, their relationship took precedence. "If we are happy, then everything will be okay." We solemnly agreed to this dose of adult medicine, since even as runners-up, we felt like the center of their world anyway.

To keep their romance alive, my parents would escape for occasional weekends, courtesy of my father's private stash that he dubbed the PAW fund. He said it stood for "Pee Away" fund, though Dad would never say "pee" or its crass cousin aloud. Every night after his day's work as service manager at a calculator company, he would drop his pocket change in a bottle, and periodically he would ask Jack and me to add up the coins. When we hit $150, he would blow it all on a getaway with Mom.

My parents were so well matched, yet so different. Mom was the more social of the two, always up on neighborhood gossip, ready to exchange phone numbers with someone she'd just met in a checkout line. She made

44

you feel as though you were the most fantastic person in the room. She glowed with equal doses of electricity and warmth. Dad cherished her enthusiasm. "Your mother has such a gift," he would say as he watched her work her magic with even the grumpiest people.

Dad's style was more understated. He defined "gentle"-man. He would quietly drop an extra quarter in the toll collector's palm to surprise the next driver in line with a free pass. He slyly decorated his hats with rivets spelling out TGFM, "Thank God for Mary." Dad was dignified, smart and well-spoken, the only father on the block who said "shan't" for "shall not" despite all his acronyms, which he used for fun. (BD, "Blame Daddy," was his favorite way to resolve any problem.)

45

"DAD SLYLY DECORATED HIS HATS WITH RIVETS SPELLING OUT TGFM, 'Thank God for Mary.'"

* * *

After a big celebration to mark their twenty-fifth anniversary, my parents decided they could no longer wait an entire year to honor their marriage. So, for the next thirty years, they designated the eleventh day of every month as their anniversary, replete with love letters and candlelit toasts. I found one note in which Mom counted the forty ways she loved Dad for forty years, including, "I still love just watching you."

Mom and Dad taught Jack and me their prescription for a good marriage: "Never go on vacation with another couple"; "Never talk about the other person's family"; and "Always assume that each of you are responsible for 51 percent of the happiness."

My parents really didn't argue much, certainly not in front of us. And if they did, Dad would drive Mom crazy with the silent treatment, which she'd break by making him laugh.

It was both inspiring and intimidating to grow up with their marriage as a role model. Like my parents (and his), Joe and I have been together for decades. I am the bigger talker and spotlight grabber while he is more low-key and thoughtful. But I highly doubt that Joe will be putting TGFML on his baseball caps.

* * *

I knew that Mom worried what would happen to Dad if she weren't around. She was the keeper of his moods and his meds. Dad was actually quite healthy most of his life, but in 1998, a stroke devastated his speech, particularly painful given his eloquence. After the stroke, we all struggled to understand him.

Mom was determined to help him speak again. As he fought to communicate, Mom was patience itself. "Ray, I know you can do it, try again, say it slow, I'm not going anywhere." I don't remember ever seeing her cry about what happened, but on a ragged piece of paper in the box, she begged, "Please help Ray speak 100% and stay well."

Inside the God Box, Mom conceded that Dad wasn't always a cooperative student. "Please keep Daddy's humor happy while recovering speech 100%." Mom kept shooting for a perfect score. She never stopped hoping that Dad's speech would return, asking again and again, "Please Jesus, give Ray back his voice. Thanks for staying near him."

* * *

I could never imagine my parents being separated, even by death. But my mom had considered the inevitable. After she died, I found an audiotape she made for Dad while

47

"I could never imagine

MY PARENTS BEING SEPARATED,
EVEN BY DEATH."

he was in a hospital for a couple of days. Having spent a lonely night staring at his empty pillow, Mom tearfully admitted that the next morning she had groggily set out two bowls for their daily cereal. That morning, on the tape, she made a vow. "I have decided that I want to die before you because I cannot bear to live without you."

Years later, the day when Mom fell ill was just a typical Friday. She awoke and told Dad she felt tired, but she dressed in her favorite blue and green colors, tossed laundry into the washer and headed out with Dad to her scheduled medical appointment. Mom was sitting next to Dad and suddenly put her hand on his knee and squeezed it and whispered, "Stay with me, Ray." Dad looked at her and could see that something was terribly wrong.

It was so like Mom to have worked it out to have a stroke in a doctor's office instead of when she was home alone watching *The Oprah Winfrey Show*. But the damage was done.

The doctor urged emergency brain surgery. Afterward, in the intensive care unit, Jack, Dad and I sat at her bedside trying to stare her into waking up. They had shaved off her lovely curls. A nurse came in carrying the kind of

49

radar gun that Target gives you to mark items for your gift registry. Every time she checked Mom's pulse or temperature, she would aim the gun at a bar code that seemed to be on Mom's ankle. All I wanted to do was scream, "Do you know who Mary Finlayson is? That she had beautiful red hair? That if she were awake, she'd be listening to you complain about your aching feet or asking to see pictures of your kids?"

* * *

As we sat, silent, in Mom's room, an aide came in and handed me a big plastic hospital bag; in it were Mom's glasses, her sandals, her blue and green outfit and a straw shoulder bag I had once bought her as a gift. I reached inside the purse and my fingers wrapped around her gold pendant–"Always together, even in Heaven." That night we moved Mom to hospice. On the drive there, the ambulance never turned on its siren. There was no need. Mom died two days later.

* * *

In the God Box, Mom had left behind a prayer for her beloved. On the back of Dad's old business card, she had written, "Dear Jesus, Please stay with my Ray." After Mom's death, it was up to me to do my part too.

I was determined to keep Dad healthy, to make him happy. I counted on my Mom-bred force of will to give me strength. I was so busy trying to be God, or at least Mom, that I barely let myself have a hard good-bye cry for the woman who taught me how to love. I threw myself into doing and saved the crying for later. Instead, I talked myself into believing that everything would be okay if I just tried hard enough.

51

compassion

Have you ever met a person who, for some reason, you feel comfortable talking to about everything, including your deepest secrets? That was my mom. She would hold your hand, look into your eyes and listen without an ounce of judgment. While she would offer advice or perspective, she also did something more. She would make a promise: "I'll put you in my God Box." And for many, that little bit of hope and validation was enough to lighten a load, if only for a moment.

My mother used to say that she attracted people with troubles, and she did–perhaps because she always appeared so welcoming and never reacted with embarrassment or shock to any disclosure. At her funeral, dozens of people came up to all of us to confide, "She was my best friend." Only on that day did the reach and depth of her relationships become apparent to us.

Later, Jack suggested that we might distribute her God Box notes to those attendees she had once mentioned by name in the box, but then Dad worried we might hurt someone's feelings if they had been left out of Mom's extensive well of prayers. I don't think anyone would have been, but Dad's concern reflected what Mom would have thought. Everyone should feel included.

* * *

Mom's compassion knew no boundaries. From hair-dressers to handymen, sullen teens to anxious retirees, Mom was the empathetic "everymother" whose support came with no strings. When I would visit her in Florida, we would head out to the Cracker Barrel for our favorite breakfast of basted eggs, and Mom would point to a server and whisper, "That's Brittany. She's married to this lousy guy who left her with four kids and she works two jobs and she is such a doll." Brittany would leave her station and come over to hug Mom like a long-lost friend.

While I'd smile at Mom over my cup of coffee, she would let her eggs grow cold as she listened to Brittany's latest mess and tell her what a good mother she was or that her hair was pretty. There were a lot of Brittanys in Mom's life. I suspect that for some of them, Mom was the only person in the world who took their problems to heart.

"MOM'S COMPASSION KNEW NO BOUNDARIES. She was the empathetic 'everymother' whose support came with no strings."

Dad would say, "Your mother has such a way with people. Do you see how she does that?" Perhaps, not too subtly, he was coaching me to mirror her. I try, but I am a shadow of Mom's warmth and sparkle, though I share her tendency to draw out people's personal stories. But the difference between Mom and me is that she would tune in and then try to help. I listen for that moment but then turn back to my own life. If a friend was sick, Mom would visit her in the hospital, help with errands, call each night to encourage and soothe. I have to admit that unless I think I can fix

55

"MOM WAS THE ONLY PERSON
IN THE WORLD WHO

took their problems
to heart."

someone's problem on the spot, I am not as personally concerned as my mom would be. To me, no one else could be.

After Mom died, and I became immersed in reading her God Box notes, I suddenly realized how many families besides ours were included. The God Box held the hopes of friends, friends of friends, relatives and strangers, like this plea for someone's great-grandchild: "Please cure Marissa Marie's heart condition. She is just a little baby."

* * *

My friend Jen wasn't thrilled about being single and buying her eleventh bridesmaid dress. Jen is Jewish, but she was intrigued when Mom put her in the box with these words, "Dear Jesus, Please let Jennie meet the right guy." (Jen later admitted,

57

"I didn't necessarily believe it would work, but I figured the more people pulling for me the better.") Soon after, she met Greg, she married him, and they had twins. After Mom died, I found a slip in the box that said, "Please cure Sue," referring to Jen's mother, a breast cancer survivor. Jen was stunned. "They never even met," she said with amazement.

Mom's God Box was even pet-friendly. In 2000, Jack and Sandy's four-year-old Chesapeake Bay retriever collapsed while the girls were at camp in Maine. The poor dog died despite Mom's note to "Please take care of poor, sick, gentle Mandy." Always the spiritual diplomat, she addressed that one to St. Francis, the patron saint of animals.

Mom's most powerful gifts were her emotional radar, which detected even unspoken hurts, and her desire to fix those hurts. In the God Box, she wrote asking for answers for a married couple who had stopped speaking to each other, for a neighbor's good blood test results, and an elderly pal afraid of losing his driver's license.

Mom's desire to help was relentless, even when she was rebuffed. Her friend Rachel used to visit and chat with her all the time. But Rachel's cancer progressed to the point

Tues Aug 1, 0*
St Francis — Please
take care of poor,
sick, gentle Mandy.
Thanks from all of us.

where she became reclusive despite Mom's attempts to coax her out for time together. "Please help my neighbor Rachel . . . she's sick and stays inside and won't talk to me."

With so many people confiding in her, and with her compassion for so many others, Mom clearly needed the God Box to play a lifesaving role for her willing but overburdened heart. Before she started the custom, Mom would keep laboring over people's problems. While her relieved friends might feel unburdened after a session with her, Mom would be left trying to make sense of what she had heard and, ultimately, trying to problem solve. "How will she ever get a job?" "What if that X-ray turns something up?" When Mom adopted the God Box, she seemed more at ease giving the problem over to stronger hands. I really believe it gave Mom true contentment and peace of mind. The release was more important than the resolution, and Mom was grateful no matter the outcome. I know that because Mom wrote "Thank you, God!" more often than anything else.

"THE RELEASE WAS MORE IMPORTANT
THAN THE RESOLUTION, AND
Mom was grateful no
matter the outcome."

* * *

Mom didn't need to use her special radar with me. During our years of talking, we were candid about pretty much everything.

Of course, I edited a bit of what I shared with her if I believed she would find it upsetting. This was easier to pull off over the phone where I could hide the expression she could always read. (How do mothers do that?) I downplayed problems, like when my ad agency was really struggling, because I didn't want her to see that I was on the brink of trouble. I didn't mind revealing the ups and downs of my friendships or even the rare disagreements with Joe, but no matter how old I was, I was still trying to score an A in positive attitude from my mom.

But there was one subject I didn't just edit; I pretended it didn't exist. Despite all we shared, Mom and I barely discussed the most obvious mother-daughter topic: children, or my lack of them. I've heard that some mothers repeatedly ask their adult children, "When am I going to have grandchildren?" Mom never did. She'd nag me about watching my weight or reducing my jammed calendar, but not about babies.

It may have been because Mom knew the heartache and the uncertainty of motherhood firsthand. When she was just twenty-three years old, she lost one of her kidneys to a serious infection. As Mom recovered in the hospital, Dad—then almost her fiancé—asked her doctor if they would be able to have children someday. The doctor advised against it. Mom and Dad married, conscious of that disappointing verdict.

But Mom wouldn't give up. She decided to defy the odds and the doctor's orders, finally giving birth to me four years later. I can only imagine how hard she must have prayed for a safe delivery. Four months later, she doubled down and became pregnant with Jack. His birth triggered an emergency hysterectomy. Though she wished for more children, Mom accepted her fate as God's will. Ironically, she was primed for her daughter's situation.

Mom kept her history to herself until I was in my forties. She broached the subject over a casual girls lunch with the odd opener, "Someday a doctor might mention that I only have one of something . . . so I want to tell you about it." For years, I took for granted that she had just put off getting pregnant on purpose. I never knew she'd risked her life to have me.

I attributed her silence on the baby front to the fact that thanks to Jack and Sandy, she already had two grandchildren to fuss over. Mom made me feel that she was happy just the way things were. She would sometimes say, "You and Joe have a good life. You can go wherever you want without being tied down. You're so lucky!"

She was right. Joe and I spent the first ten years of our

married life just enjoying our time as a couple. But when we were in our late thirties, we went through four years of fertility treatments, though I suppose it ought to have been called infertility. While sneaking off to the frequent tests and needles and enduring the longest months of my life, I never told anyone at my office. I didn't even tell Mom. I didn't want her to think that anything was wrong with me. I knew she would start doing research and then worry that I would overdo the intervention. Nothing worked, and after one final procedure, I said "enough," and truly, Joe and I were enough.

All that time I kept it between Joe and me, naively hoping I would break the silence with a big surprise announcement that never came. It was a long and lonely wait.

But now, Mom was speaking to me. On a second round of reviewing the notes in the ten boxes, I noticed a piece of flowered stationery that I had bypassed earlier, a happy thank-you note I had written to my parents. Mom must have placed it in there because it cheered her. I stared at it more closely this time, and there in the margin, next to my own writing, Mom had added this one simple sentence: "Sweet mother, Sweet Jesus, if it's right, a child for

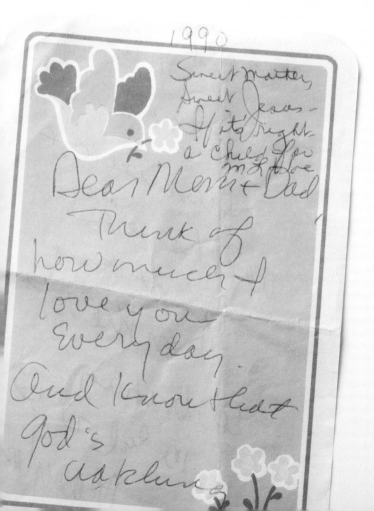

Mary Lou and Joe." It was dated 1990 when we had hit our wall. Her emotional radar had succeeded once again.

How many nights had she fallen asleep wondering if I were pregnant or searched for a clue in my eyes as I held my nieces? Did she and Dad debate whether to bring it up? By keeping her prayers between herself and God, Mom spared me feeling that I had failed her in any way. She may have been disappointed, but after reading that single line in the note from the God Box, I knew she had accepted whatever was meant to be. And I loved her even more.

* * *

My mother knew when to listen and when to pray and when to help. I wonder how many people never knew the compassion Mary Finlayson held for them and how hard, in the privacy of her God Box, she prayed for them and their struggles.

"My mother
knew when
to listen
AND WHEN TO PRAY

AND WHEN TO HELP."

aspiration

Many of the God Box entries were hard to decipher, thanks to my mother's years of taking dictation during the heyday of shorthand. But her passion was always loud and clear, especially when she wrote about my career. Mom and I were bonded by our drive to succeed, to make a mark, to contribute.

* * *

My mother was a working woman all her life. Her first job was as a secretary at the Philadelphia Navy Yard, and her first boss was a young officer named Richard Nixon. Yes, *the* Richard Nixon. He was Mom's claim to fame in stories she told Jack and me when we were growing up. As she recalled, "He was so charming and handsome and he was so in love with Pat." Mom was ticked when Watergate ruined her best story.

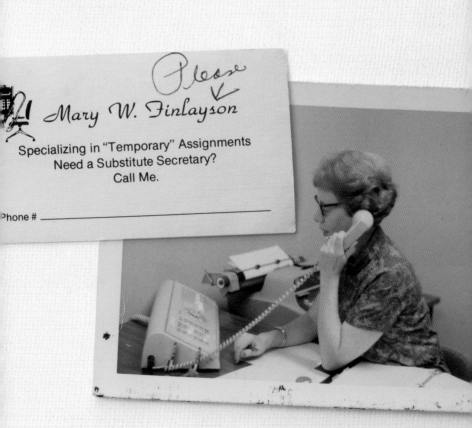

Mary W. Finlayson

Please ✓

Specializing in "Temporary" Assignments
Need a Substitute Secretary?
Call Me.

Phone # _____

"You can do and be anything, BUT NO MATTER WHAT YOU CHOOSE TO DO, WE WILL LOVE YOU JUST THE SAME."

Over the years, Mom worked as a secretary and office manager in dozens of companies in downtown Philadelphia. She was a whiz with a keyboard, a charmer on the phone. Mom loved heading out to her job every day, but her redhead's temperament made her a flight risk. Within the first couple of hours at a new assignment, if her new office mates were nasty, she would phone Dad to say, "Ray, pick me up at lunchtime. I'm not going back." She refused to trade her peace of mind for a paycheck, even though she needed it. She would rather risk finding another job than lose her ability to be joyful and calm with her family at the end of the day. I was forty-five years old before I had the guts to recognize the importance of that trade-off.

Mom's favorite jobs were in ad agencies. Every night at the dinner table she would entertain us with the juicy details of glamorous photo shoots, office intrigue and creative catfights. Her tales from the office were my first taste of the career I hoped to have one day.

Mom's enthusiasm for her 9-to-5 life far outshone her interest in the kitchen. Our house was neat, our lunch bags were packed each night, but Mom was more Lois Lane than Betty Crocker. Our weekly menus were a

71

rerun of Ragu and spaghetti, Velveeta and elbow macaroni, Shake 'n Bake chicken, and whatever Mom cooked in advance. After school, Jack and I were in charge of thawing something for dinner. We would open the freezer and find Tupperware containers Mom had labeled with peel-off paper name tags filled in with "Hi, my name is Meatballs" or "Hello, I'm Macaroni and Cheese."

*   *   *

Jack and I were encouraged to excel from the get-go. Besides Mom's dinner table tutorials, I remember Dad teaching us his Dale Carnegie speaking techniques. Even as kids, Jack and I were expected to stand and deliver the presentation, repeating it back to him and using our most expressive body language to make the sale.

Both of our parents took us to the office before "Take Your Daughter or Son to Work Day" even existed. Mom coached Jack and me to dream big with her refrain of "You can do and be anything," always followed by, "But no matter what you choose to do, we will love you just the same." Her high expectations fueled our ambitions, but her unconditional love reassured us that even if we failed, we would never be failures in her eyes. What a gift to a child.

As a result, our self-esteem was already going full steam by an early age. Perhaps mine was even in over-drive. In fifth grade, for example, the teacher called me to the front of the classroom, which was not unusual considering the grades I was pulling down. I thought I was about to receive a surprise award. Instead, the nun stared down at me and asked, "Do you know what the word *conceited* means?" She clicked her rosary beads as I looked up at her. "No, Sister," I answered. "Well, then, go home and look it up in the dictionary, and tell your mother that's what I said you are." Some of the other kids giggled, so I knew it wasn't good. After school, when I discovered what the word meant, I was appalled. So was Mom. "How dare she say that? You're fine just the way you are."

I don't remember her challenging the nun, but I knew Mom was on my side. She always was.

* * *

Mom continued to work even after Dad retired. She wasn't afraid to try anything, even in her seventies. She promoted her services as a temporary secretary. I found one of her business cards in the God Box with a handwritten plea of "Please!" on the front.

She created and taught a night course at the local high school for women returning to the workforce. She price-tagged donations at the church thrift shop, answered the phone for a cement mixing yard and managed the affairs of a wealthy invalid. She loved earning her own "pin money," as she called it, and it was her excuse for not playing golf or learning how to play bridge. "Too booooring!" she'd laugh.

*　*　*

Despite her own busy career, Mom's favorite job was keeping track of her children's on our nightly phone calls. I was shocked how often she dispatched everything Jack and I reported straight to the God Box, her one-stop career counseling center.

74

Thanks to Mom, I had followed in her footsteps, eventually joining the advertising business, first as an agency account supervisor and finally becoming CEO of a big New York firm. I was ambitious, driven and single-mindedly focused on success. On my frequent flights, I was all business–no patience in the security line, no chats with seatmates, hanging on my cell phone till the last available moment. I was a woman on a mission to win. Mom was proud of each promotion and urged me forward every step of the way, with God Box entries such as, "If it's right, let Mary Lou win the Avon advertising account." I did.

Elsewhere in the God Box, I would find the names of dozens of new business wins cheered on by Mom. One spring, for instance, she wrote on a folded napkin the names of six companies I was pitching, as though it were a heavenly hit list. On the back of a Ruby Tuesday's coaster, Mom even alerted God to the exact time I was making my presentation: "Liberty Mutual, 4 p.m., Friday April 3, 1998." It turned out she was toasting my victory prematurely during a 2-for-1 happy hour since that win wasn't meant to be. "Meant to be" was the verdict Mom and I applied to both good and bad outcomes because, despite our self-confidence, we believed that God cast the final vote. As much as I acted as if I could move mountains with my willpower, like thinking I could force a new business win, I knew I wasn't really in charge of anything. Deep inside, I believed that God was. But oh, how I tried.

* * *

During our long-distance phone calls, I complained to Mom about office politics quite a bit. Would I get a bonus? Would I work out a disagreement? No matter the issue, she

always had my back and was unafraid
to take on my adversaries in the God
Box. She even put a hex on some of
my nastier coworkers: "Dear God, Get
rid of (Blank) and (Blank). They're
mean to ML." I haven't revealed their
names here, but Mom turned them in
to the Higher Authority upstairs.

Jack's career path–from promo-
tions to relocations to company buy-
outs–was detailed in the God Box as
well. On one side of a piece of torn
notepaper, Mom had scratched out a
business quandary of Jack's and on
the other, her Home Depot shopping
list for petunias and fertilizer. (She
often wrote requests on the run.) Big
worries were stashed right alongside
the small. When Jack was considering
a move to Hong Kong, Mom prayed,
"Please let Jack and Sandy be in uni-
son for change of jobs. Decision under

"She always had my back AND WAS UNAFRAID TO TAKE ON MY ADVERSARIES IN THE GOD BOX."

5 days." I knew this was Mom's code for "Please don't let them move a million miles away from me!" They didn't.

Mom even let Jack write a couple of job-related petitions himself. She knew that writing things down would ease his anxiety and, perhaps, lure him back to the faith (again!). For his part, Jack appreciated the God Box because he knew it gave Mom comfort, like a security blanket for her and for anyone mentioned on the notes inside.

* * *

Mom was so unabashedly proud of Jack and me that she set up a sort of shrine to us in her bedroom. On either side of the TV, she hung huge framed corporate photos of us clad in requisite dark suits, our hands folded in that "I'm in charge but I'm a nice person" pose. She used to say that she fell asleep looking at our faces in between glances at her favorite old movies.

Mom's entreaties on our behalf were mostly about getting ahead and achieving the next big goal. So I was amazed to see what Mom wrote on June 14, 1998, on the front of my business card as president of the New York ad agency I mentioned earlier. "Please Jesus, a new job for Mary Lou." Looking at that business card, one would think I already

May '98
Pray for JACK & Sandy to
be _____ ison for charge
o _____ _____ under ⑤

Please, Jesus, You'd the
right job. Change for
Jackie. He's a good son &
a very hardworker,

5/24
Jesus,
31 pages
this week
is coming f
u. I feel u.

4/1/06 New and
hetter job for Jack
please!

327-4727
NS • SAN FRANCISCO • SAN JOSE

Dec 2005

from the desk of

/local

ch/since
ck-new
ept 9 &
Help other
so did Youn

had a good enough job and my mom would be thrilled for me after all her years of typing ad copy and making coffee.

But Mom knew what I wouldn't admit. By 1998, I was exhausted from overworking and under-living. The hours were punishing and the pressure to stay on top unforgiving. I was so stressed that I used to fantasize about getting hit by a taxi and breaking a leg so I'd be laid up and no one could bother me for a month or so.

But how could I quit when she was so proud of me? Whenever I got down about a bad day and threatened to walk, she'd remind me how lucky I was to have such a big job or convince me that things would improve. "Just get a good night's sleep and tomorrow will be better." I'd try to follow her advice and then wake up at 2:00 a.m. to stare at the clock and worry. I was losing my patience, my humor and, most of all, my passion for something I had once loved. But, to me, giving up was akin to failure and therefore not an option I would entertain.

I felt that I couldn't tell Mom how miserable I really was. But I didn't have to. I found several notes dated from that period where Mom asked repeatedly for my relief from my distress. A friend saw that I was going through the mental gymnastics of trying not to quit yet wishing desperately I could, and she finally convinced me I could just declare a time-out from my overblown agenda. I took her advice and got up the nerve to request a short leave. When I called my Mom to tell her the news, she cried with joy for her answered prayers.

*   *   *

My last eight years with Mom were the most creative of my career. I founded a small company dedicated to understanding women by listening deeply to them, a talent I'd inherited from Mom. Mary Finlayson was on the case. "Please help Mary Lou's business succeed," she wrote. "She only wants to help make people better."

When I wrote my first book, Mom tapped her upstairs connections in the God Box: "Please let Mary Lou's book be a success." Of course, Mom expected it to be a blockbuster and asked God to do some heavy lifting for the launch. "Oprah Winfrey, Diane Sawyer, The View. Please Jesus, let Mary Lou get on these shows with her book." (For the record, Mom eventually scored two out of three.)

Though I knew it all along, the God Box proved that

Mom was my steadiest business partner. She gloried in my wins, she ached for my losses. She was so, so proud.

Mom used to say I was "the wind beneath her wings," an image taken from the lyrics of the theme song of our favorite chick flick, *Beaches*. In truth, it was the other way around. She was *my* hero. How could I not soar when my mother believed I could fly? How could I be afraid, knowing she loved me even if I fell?

perseverance

I am the daughter of a woman who never gave up trying. Never. If I expressed doubts about my ability to complete a task or make the grade, Mom had one response: "Can't means won't." She refused to be knocked out of the game by life's problems. Hurtful comments, lost keys, negative blood tests–nothing threw her off course. That can-do determination spilled over to Dad, Jack and me, so much so that others might have thought the Finlaysons never had a cloudy day. But that wasn't true. The difference, thanks to Mom, was that during those difficult days, we didn't take time to dwell on the negative. We were too busy searching for the silver lining.

That Mom kept up her God Box ritual for twenty years testifies to her perseverance. Even though she was quick to quit a testy job, she never gave up on any concern of

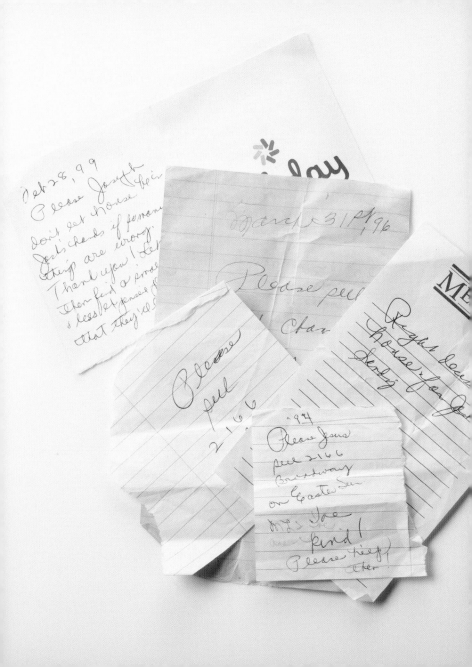

her family and friends, and that dogged determination threaded through her years of handwritten missives. During the years when she worried the most–as in 1998, which was bulging with notes about my stressful job–her words adopted a machine-gun-like persistence, asking again and again for an answer from God.

Mom's ability to barrel through troubles wasn't limited to big issues like job crises or health problems. She was relentless even with life's small bumps. For example, she was a tiger on the issue of buying and selling houses. When Joe and I were trying to sell our apartment in New York in a down market, Mom turned to her real estate expert on high, St. Joseph. Convinced he would score a sale if we buried his statue in the front lawn, but knowing we couldn't do so under a Manhattan sidewalk, she expected results nevertheless: "Please sell 2166 Broadway." A month later, thinking she might need to send a reminder since no buyers had yet appeared, Mom tried another tack: "Please sell 2166 Broadway on Easter Sunday."

When Mom was noodling a tiny worry in her mind, she would submit a plea multiple times, just

April 28, 99 Please give us good health is good cruise make Dad happy on Cruise. Let Bingo flow the right place. I love you, Jesus

Please choose correct cabin + ship for "kids' cruise (mothers Day '99) I love you, dearest Jesus

5/16/99 Thanks Jesus for perfect Royal Caribbean cruise for 50th & the best family in their world. Love, you, Lea

to be sure she'd been heard. When Jack, Sandy, Joe and I chipped in for a Mother's Day cruise for my parents in 1999, Mom wrote three petitions in one month for help in choosing the right cabin. I suppose that if the cruise line had assigned them a poorly located room, she'd have sent God semaphore signals from the high seas.

She was persistent.

* * *

On the subject of our family's health, Mom pulled out all the stops. If the God Box were a phone line to Heaven, Mom would have had the health division on speed dial because she was Dr. Mom in a family that acted as if sickness could be wished away.

Dad was the architect of the Finlayson "never sick" policy. Mom used to tease that Dad was a Christian

Scientist; we had no idea what that meant, except that we were supposed to ignore illness. He loved us so much, especially Mom, that he didn't want anything to ever be wrong.

Dad was the king of mind over matter. He joked about his "trick knee" his whole life until an MRI pinpointed severe arthritis, chronic since the 1930s. He brushed off his stroke as just an annoyance. Though he lost his natural ease with speaking, Dad insisted on stretching for the more challenging word–for example, "lugubrious" for "sad"–even if he had to sound it out a syllable at a time. Jack and I did our best to live up to his wellness standards, with perfect attendance nearly every year of grammar school. Did we unknowingly pass the chicken pox around?

87

Jack and I bought into Dad's "never sick" policy, but Mom had a harder time with it. She wanted her turn to be sick now and then.

I remember, for example, that the first winter my parents visited Joe and me in New York, Mom sprained her ankle on a curb. Dad's remedy for the ride home to Philadelphia was to wedge her foot out the window into a brewing sleet storm. He figured that chilling her raised ankle would do the trick by exit 8 on the New Jersey Turnpike. A few days later, Dad suggested that Mom walk outdoors to get her mobility back. Reluctantly, Mom hobbled to the door, took one step off the front porch and promptly sprained her other ankle. Let's just say it wasn't a high point in our family's medical history.

So, with sympathy in short supply, Mom turned to her own inventive, preventive care. She was our family's disease detector. We would constantly switch seats in a restaurant because my mother worried about catching a cold from the draught of ceiling fans. At church, she watched out for anyone who sneezed before the "kiss of peace" ceremony and would duck her head into her handbag rather than chance a germ-filled handshake.

For most of our lives, we were lucky enough not to have too many major illnesses to test our perseverance. Despite her off and on allergies and occasional flu, Mom, ever cheerful, was buying into our cult of wellness—or so we assumed. But once opened, the God Box called our bluff. The little scraps told a different story. Even though we had listened to Mom's various symptoms and worries, we hadn't appreciated at the time how much she kept inside as she powered through.

Inside the God Box, Mom kept a running journal of all the illnesses she endured so that she could keep up her mothering without complaint. "Please control my blood pressure. I need to take care of my family." "Please let this new mole on my right arm be taken away so I can still work for you."

The God Box served as the sympathetic healer that Mom needed on earth. She thanked God for every positive checkup and averted close call. After a collision with Jack's playful dog, Mom wrote, "Thanks for protecting me when I fell. Love, Mary." And then, in case God didn't notice her spill, "P.S., fell against kitchen counter." But such incidents were small stuff compared to the news that would put her fortitude to the test.

* * *

A few years after moving to Florida, Mom was diagnosed with a rare and incurable blood cancer called mylefibrosis, where red and white blood cell counts get out of whack and eventually weaken a person to death. Mom endured transfusions and chemotherapy drugs for almost twenty

"Mom's faith never flagged. SHE NEVER STOPPED HOPING FOR A CURE OR A MIRACLE."

```
Memorial Day 1994

Dearest Jesus,

Please hear me.  My mouth is so very sore.  Please cure it,
and cure my platlet problem.  I thank you, and I love you.

Mary
```

years, outliving the odds. Yet, because of our "never sick" policy, Mom never revealed that news to anyone but us rather than evoke (and have to endure) despairing reactions from others. She always said she hated it when people jumped to the darkest conclusions—"Darn crepehangers!"

The God Box was also a way for Mom to talk about what hurt rather than complain to her beloved husband. "Please help me. Ray doesn't want to hear that I'm sick," she wrote in secret. Safe inside, she cried to those slips of paper, year after year.

Memorial Day 1994: "Please hear me. My mouth is very sore. Please cure it and cure my platelet problem. I thank you and I love you."

July 6, 2000: "My dearest Ray cannot bear to see me (like this). These past days make me feel weak, tired and just miserable. You have answered so many of my requests for my family. Help the Dr. find an answer."

March 2003: "Please, God (give me) the answer to restoring red blood cells."

The disease got worse and worse, but despite the debilitating effects of her treatments, Mom showed only her sunny side to her friends and family. And Mom's faith never flagged, nor did she ever stop praying for a cure or a miracle. When she had that deadly stroke, she was in her hematologist's office hoping for better news.

Jack and I–and especially Dad– felt awful when we read those notes. Until then, we hadn't truly grasped just how intensely she had suffered.

* * *

Three years after Mom died, I got my own experience with something I couldn't wish away. My routine mammogram turned up early stage breast cancer. My first instinct was to revert to the family tradition and tell no one except Joe, Jack, Sandy and Dad. Like Mom, I didn't want to

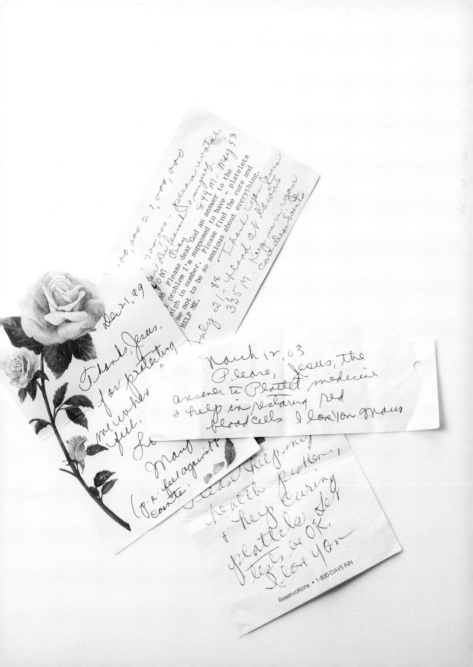

Dec 21,99

,000,000 = 1,000,000
,000,000 = 1,000,000
2 M Arkansas Reservation.
88 M Oregon Reservation.
5.49 M. May 53

Please dear God an answer to the
problem I'm supposed to have - platelets
high in number. Please find the cure and
me not to be so anxious about everything.
HELP ME.

July 21, 48   Thank you
335 M. Kansas   God & Jesus
                 and Days Santa

Thank Jesus,
for protecting
my other
yield.
Lo
     Mary
(P.S. feel against
contse.

March 12, 03
   Please, Jesus, the
answer to Platlet mediceni
+ help in restoring red
   blood cells. I love You Mous

Please help my
health problem,
+ keep curing
yplatlets step
feel, or OK.
I love You

Reservations • 1-800-DAYS INN

be on the receiving end of anyone's pity, despite wanting others' support. After years of practicing silence through the fertility process, I figured I would just go it alone.

After surgery, I was scheduled for thirty-three days of radiation. I got a manicure, had my hair styled, and walked into the hospital like I was showing up for a premiere.

I lay down on a big steel table in the crosshairs of the radiation machine. The technicians ordered me not to move or breathe. I was so scared I couldn't anyway. All I wanted was Mom. As the radiation blared, tears streamed down my face.

That first day, I made a decision. I would do what Mom would do. I would use this time to become radiant, inside and out, not radiated. But without her, I needed some company for the journey. I slowly started to share the news with some of my closest friends and neighbors, who gave me a rush of support I never could have imagined: everything from a cup of coffee in the park after a treatment to a Sunday afternoon walk to cry if I wanted to so I could buck up for the following week. I felt incredibly energized thanks to getting it off my chest, so to speak, though Mom would never have approved of being so public.

*   *   *

After Mom's funeral, Jack and I did whatever we could to distract ourselves from our grief. Jack sorted through Dad's bills. I started to write thank-you notes on his behalf. We spoke with neighbors who stopped in to share condolences. But most of the time Dad just sat in his recliner or took naps, trying to escape the deafening silence that Mom had left behind.

I knew we all had to get out of the lonely Florida house, and I had just the solution. I had been preparing a renovation project to expand our house in Pennsylvania. I had shared the blueprints with Dad and dubbed him my "house whisperer" because he had such a talent for design and problem solving.

I knew that he would love to be on-site as my personal foreman. He lit up at the idea of a change of scene, so we flew back north to throw our battered hearts into building fever.

I was still shaky after losing Mom, but I put on a cheerful front for my father. Dad was eighty-eight years old and suffering the lingering effects of his stroke, yet his resilience was remarkable. We joined in the barn raising,

"DURING THE SUMMER MONTHS THAT FOLLOWED,
the project became
a shared tonic for
Dad and me."

wielding wooden mallets to pound in the pegs, grabbing the rope line with the crew to give our tug to the frame.

When I look at pictures of that event, held just two weeks after the loss of Mom, I am amazed at the grit and the joy on our faces. During the summer months that followed, the project became a shared tonic for Dad and me. We worked to create a garden dedicated to Mom. We called it "The Sanctuary." Dad encouraged me to place my writing desk in a spot where I could look out on the garden and think of her.

Most of that summer I kept up a bright face for everyone. But when you're the crier in the family, it's hard to hide the tears. If I filled up with memories of Mom, Dad would shake his head and ask me to be happy–"She'd want you to be"–and Jack would reassure me that she was in Heaven and not suffering any more. Joe would hold me in his arms when I lost it, but he couldn't find the words to say. Finally, a good friend suggested, "Sometime, when everyone is out of the house, take a hot shower and bawl your eyes out." I did. Under the pounding water, I broke down in sobs, asking, "Why did you leave me?" and proclaiming, "I want you back. I miss you so much. I hate when people say you're in a better place. A better place would be with me." Toweling off, I have to admit I felt better, if only because I felt ready to be strong again.

By September, Dad wanted to return to Florida. He always told us, "I never want to be a burden to my kids," and he stuck to his guns. As hard as it was to think of him there alone, we supported his decision.

But through it all, I mostly counted on my own self-determined force and I never thought to ask for help in the God Box, as Mom had done. I don't know why I didn't give it a try except that it was her way of coping, not mine. Without Mom, I had to go forward my own way, one foot in front of the other. Her God Boxes–some still in Florida, some up north–just gathered dust.

letting go

As the months passed, our lives moved along. Jack became CEO of a tech company, and he and Sandy kept their girls focused on academics as Kelley went to college and Meghan started high school. Joe and I celebrated our thirtieth anniversary, and I started to write the first book of mine that Mom would never read. Dad flew back south alone.

Every month, Jack and I took turns visiting Dad in Florida. On one of my first flights there, I sat next to an elderly woman. She turned to me and asked, "Are you headed home to Fort Myers or do you live in New York?" My radio silence reflex was about to kick in, but I looked at her expectant face and said, "My parents live in Florida. Well, my Dad does. I lost my Mom." I filled with tears and she grabbed my hand and started to talk to me about how much she missed her own long-distance daughter. We chatted most of the flight. Was I becoming my mother?

During my visits, Dad and I would dress up and go out to dinner at a local oyster house. We'd order the hottest cocktail sauce and slurp to our hearts' content. I started to loosen up, chatting with the hostess and the waitresses, listening to their stories. Since I was no better at cooking than Mom had been, I served Dad takeout meals on his porch, but always with candlelight and his favorite music, as Mom would have done.

I felt my job was to keep Dad happy and well. That's what I had promised Mom. But Dad was doing his own part too.

"I FELT MY JOB WAS TO KEEP DAD HAPPY AND WELL. That's what I had promised Mom."

* * *

During that summer we spent house-building, perhaps because we felt such an emotional vacuum without Mom, Dad and I started bonding with the construction team. Dad especially took to the general contractor, Chuck, who was remarkably like Mom in his enthusiasm and passion. Chuck taught Dad the gesture of "Namaste," the simple folding of hands to salute the inner goodness in others. Dad, whose speech had become harder to understand, started Namaste-ing everyone: from his favorite waitress, Pearl, to the pest control guy when he came to the door, to our King Charles spaniel, DannyBoy. The sight of my tall, white-haired, reserved Dad bowing and smiling at strangers was so sweet to witness.

Once back in Florida, Dad kept warming up. He told me that one day while he was sitting alone in front of his garage, his neighbor Meg walked over to him and said, "I need a hug." Dad said, "So do I." That big hug became the first of many for Dad, who had often admitted, "I've never been a hugger." Mom was. I started to see Dad make friends in a way he had never done before.

Still, Dad's happiness was my number one job, assigned by Mom. I felt that if I could stay in control of his health and his humor, if I were as vigilant as Mom had been, I could solve anything that happened to Dad. Lisa, long a friend of my mom's, would visit each day to bring Dad food and to chat about her job. I called her my

"Southern sister," and she'd keep us up on Dad's spirits day to day.

But in early March 2010, just before dawn, Dad fell. I flew to Florida, planning to make him better again. An MRI told a different story. A tumor that had begun as undetected kidney cancer had spread to his brain. I brought him home from the hospital, wishing that the news wasn't so awful, hating to be the one to let him know.

Out on his porch after dinner, Dad asked me to be straight with him. "How long?"

"Six weeks," I answered.

His eyes filled up and he asked for a moment alone. He stood up and pushed his walker into the living room where he sat in his recliner to think.

I immediately began making plans to take him home with me, but Dad had no intention of going north and quipped that the only way he was leaving Florida was in a hearse. But he relented when Jack called and begged him to be near his grandkids. "Alright," he conceded reluctantly, "it's expensive flying up there, but it's free flying out."

* * *

I set up Dad with hospice in our Pennsylvania house, where Jack and Sandy could often join me and Joe and Stacia, a caring aide, to help, to talk, to just be by Dad's side.

Day by day he was losing weight but not his humor. The first time I had to give him morphine, I was really nervous. I injected some into vanilla pudding. I gave him the bowl and Dad carefully took a spoonful. He looked at me. I stared back. Then, dramatically, he dropped the spoon, slumped in his chair, tongue out, faking his own death. I almost passed out, first from shock, then from laughing.

Jack and I were side by side through it all. As hard as it was, we loved that sacred time together with our father. But Dad really just wanted to be with Mom. Four years of missing her were more than enough. Jack asked, "Do you think that you will see Mom in Heaven?" And Dad nodded firmly. "Will she be the age she was when you last saw her?" Jack continued. Dad smiled and we leaned in close to make out his answer: "I never really thought about that. Wouldn't matter . . . she would be well . . . and happy." That's how I pictured my parents, smiling and dancing the way I imagined they did on the night they met. Dad would gently hold Mom's hand as though it were glass . . . his other hand firmly on her back, and they'd foxtrot into their dream world.

> ## "As hard as it was, JACK
> AND I LOVED THAT SACRED TIME TOGETHER
> WITH OUR FATHER."

The days and nights after that were the hardest. Dad was rarely awake, but often restless. One night when he was confused and resisting my clumsy attempt to give him morphine, I got so upset I ran out of the house, screaming to the night sky, "I'm his daughter, not his doctor!" I just didn't know what to do. When I came back inside, Dad was calmer and I sat on his bed. He took my hand in his and said, "I feel so sad for you." I could barely get out the words, "I feel sad for both of us, Daddy."

Watching and waiting, helpless, was tearing me up inside. I couldn't fix him. But I couldn't let him go.

One April afternoon, alone with Dad, I sat nearby, watching him breathe. He seemed so far away. And I knew there was only one person who would know what to do.

Desperate, I grabbed a piece of lined yellow paper and began writing. "Dear Jesus (and Mom), I think it's time to take Daddy back home. He has been such a strong and loving father, devoted husband, dear and generous friend to so many people for so many years . . . But I see how tired and frail he is . . . I never thought I could ask this . . . but please bring Daddy to Heaven, to your arms.

"I NEVER THOUGHT
I COULD ASK THIS . . .
but please
bring Daddy
to Heaven."

105

I folded it up small and went upstairs to place it in one of Mom's old God Boxes. I truly felt her calming hand on mine. My heart finally lifted. My father died peacefully three days later. Jack was with him when it happened. I believe Dad knew I had kissed him good-bye.

* * *

"Watching and waiting, helpless, WAS TEARING ME UP INSIDE. I KNEW THERE WAS ONLY ONE PERSON WHO WOULD KNOW WHAT TO DO."

April 17, 2010

Dear Jesus (and Mom),

I think it's time to take Daddy back home. He has been such a strong and loving father, devoted husband, dear and generous friend to so many people for so many years.

I know that you don't want him to be in pain... that maybe you are letting me be part of this sacred ritual so that I can let him go. Because if Daddy were still teasing me + talking to me and hugging me, how could I give him back.

But I see how tired and frail he is. He has done your work on earth to the best of his heart + strength + soul. I never thought I could ask this... but please bring Daddy to Heaven. to your arms. And someday. I will join you in love. Always together, even in heaven. Always Dad's girl, Mary Lou

That letter to God and Mom became the first message in what is now my own God Box. I decided to move it to one of the boxes I had given my mother, one she thought was too fancy. It's just a simple oval wood one, engraved with a beautiful quote from Sarah Josepha Hale: "There is no influence so powerful as that of a mother."

When someone's in trouble, I try to remember to write things down and put the notes inside the box. I find that I turn to my God Box more for the big worries, like praying for my cousin who underwent a lung transplant or a friend who's going through a divorce. But each time I place a slip of paper inside, I honestly feel the beginnings of that relief that was so precious to Mom.

Unlike Mom, I leave my box out on a table so I can tell people about the ritual and about her. Sometimes friends who know the story ask if they can tuck in petitions for themselves. They tell me that they address some of them to God and others to "Dear Mary." We figure she can pass them right along.

* * *

Today I see a different person in the mirror from the woman who was more polite than warm, more determined than generous. I have more friends now than I ever had. Last Christmas, my first without either Mom or Dad, Joe and I decided to invite twenty-five friends to a pot-luck dinner at our home. I fussed over the decorations and menu and then lost myself in the mess and the joyful chaos in the kitchen. Everyone took over. I just went with it. I always knew them as neighbors, but now I know their stories. I've been by their side through their disappoint-ments and celebrations. Instead of simply nodding, I really listen and try to help. Maybe this is what it felt like to be Mom. Maybe this was the gift she tried so hard to give.

And now when I find myself in the middle of a situa-tion that is negative or hurtful, I'm better at stepping away and letting it go. When I fall back to my habit of overdoing, I ask Joe to rescue me, which is my own way of saying, "Can you pick me up? I'm not going back there."

And as time goes by, I talk more often to Mom. I can hear her voice in my head if I let myself listen. I can imitate just what she'd say, the kind of good advice I remember from growing up: "God closes a door, He opens a win-dow." Her words are gifts that she gives me all over again.

It might sound odd, but when I am feeling alone or

afraid, I will sometimes reach into my coat pocket and find a holy card or a rosary she placed there long ago. Last Christmas, inside a box of dusty decorations, I found an unopened greeting card that she had sent to me years before. She had written, "I love you, Anna Banana." I swear she knows when I need her most.

No matter the season, I love to sit in The Sanctuary, the garden Dad and I dedicated to Mom and planted with hostas and birch trees and a scarlet azalea because she was allergic to roses. At the center of the garden is a stone bench, created from a piece of weathered river stone found near our home. On the bench are carved the words from the pendant Mom wore over her heart all those years: "Always together, even in Heaven." The stone's surface had naturally worn into two gentle slopes, as if a pair of friends had sat on it together chatting for centuries. When I need to feel her presence, I sit on one side of that bench and pretend she's next to me. Whenever I have a wish or a worry, I turn to her for advice. The words she taught me come back as clear as can be: it doesn't hurt to ask.

I'll never, ever stop being her daughter.

Hands on.

"ON THE BENCH ARE CARVED
THE WORDS FROM THE PENDANT
MOM WORE OVER HER HEART
ALL THOSE YEARS:
'Always together,
even in
Heaven.'"

"NO MATTER WHAT
YOU DO,
EVEN IF YOU SIMPLY
SHARE THIS STORY
WITH A FRIEND,
you will
take
Mary's
gift
forward."

you

I hope this story of my mother's God Box ritual might inspire you to begin the practice of keeping your own. The idea is to surrender your wishes, worries and decisions in the way that works best for you and your life.

People often ask me, "How do I begin?" or "Where do I find the perfect box?" I suggest that, as my mother did, you let your own God Box be free of any restrictions. If a pretty box is important to you, that's wonderful. But a simple box of any kind will do. The same holds true for the paper. If you are a fan of beautiful stationery, then enjoy. But what made the God Box work so well for Mom is that she used what-ever paper was nearby so she could get her message quickly into the box and off her mind. She felt that approach made it easier to keep a promise during a busy day since her note writing was very spontaneous and from her heart.

I have heard stories of those who place their intentions in a book or in a drawer. What's more important is that you choose what fits you, your beliefs, your life. And you may find that looking back through your messages from time to time will teach you a little about yourself. You'll observe how much you worry or hope, whom you pray for most often and how your petitions are resolved, as they are meant to be.

And although I don't believe that my mom kept her God Boxes for us to find as proof of her devotion to us, it's certainly become a wonderful legacy for my family. Perhaps that motivation will encourage you to start one for your own family to have someday.

You can learn more about this book and find special content about the God Box on my website: theGodBoxproject.com. If you'd like to share your God Box experience with others, I would love to hear from you as you create your own practice. I'll be telling more stories there, as the God Box finds its way around the world. You can also find me on Facebook at The God Box Project. If you are active on Twitter, check out @GodBoxProject (#GodBoxProject) for updates too.

If you find apps a useful way to stay on top of your intentions as you move through your busy days, The God Box app will be available on iTunes. There you can both insert your concerns into a virtual box as well as send an email to the person in your thoughts, letting them know "You're in my God Box." Sometimes just telling someone you remembered to care is cure in itself.

When you begin the process, you may find it's something you do every day or that you are a little more sporadic with your requests. Remember that the hardest part, letting go, takes time. I am still learning too. But I believe that you will find comfort and hope in this simple gesture of faith and release.

115

One more way to experience "The God Box" is to attend a performance of my one woman play "The God Box, A Daughter's Story." Though I grew up as a hopeful dancer and actress, long ago I had set aside my childhood dreams. My father had wisely advised, "Theater will be your avocation." I didn't know what he meant at the time, but as my grown up life grew busier, I understood. Still, my years of speaking on stages around the world kept the theater bug alive inside.

While writing this book, I decided to collaborate with a seasoned NYC director/actor/playwright Martha Wollner to evolve "The God Box" to a live theater event. Developing the script revealed new stories—both funny and sad—of my journey of love and letting go. The result is a one hour theatrical piece that I am performing around the country. Proceeds from tickets and book sales go directly to local cancer care, hospice, healthcare and women's organizations. I love touching communities with this story of faith and family and giving back to honor Mom's memory. Learn more at theGodBoxproject.com/performance.

No matter what you do, even if you simply share this story with a friend, you will have taken Mary's gift forward. And that is a prayer answered. She'd ask for nothing more.

acknowledgments

I nside my own God Box, I've placed the names of these amazing people who have given their talent to this labor of love. I first want to acknowledge Kristin van Ogtrop and Noelle Howey of *Real Simple* magazine for believing in my story from the beginning.

I have been thrilled to work with a team that spans the globe but shares one thing in common: a personal connection to the hope embedded in my mom's simple ritual. I send my heartfelt thanks to marketing strategist and creative director Lissa Lowe; creative collaborators Jennie Willink and Susan Kittenplan of Will/Plan Projects; graphic designer Rachel Cost; illustrator Kathryn Whyte; photographer Mark Laita; filmmakers Kristin Brewer and Michael Sullivan of Taproot Films; filmmakers David Broad and Tony Chow of Left of Frame; Jude Lutge and

Julie Vetter of Hoi Moon Marketing; Peter Mack and Phillip Ting of Elephant Ideas & Design; Beth Feldman and the team from K2 Kommunications; editors Lari Bishop and Linda O'Doughda, designer Sheila Parr, and production manager Bryan Carroll of Greenleaf Book Group; singer/songwriter Aron Wright; and theatrical director Martha Wollner. Special appreciation to my Just Ask a Woman team, Chelsea Castner, Tracy Chapman and Jen Drexler, and Nancy Berk, Colleen Tomko, Honora Gilmore, Valerie Sherman and the many, many friends who have encouraged me throughout this journey.

I was honored to have many generous caregivers who were by Mom and Dad's side when we needed them most. My deep thanks to our Ft. Myers, Florida supporters including Dr. James Reeves, our friends, Lisa Hoefling, Irene Marti, Meg and Marge Williams and the staff of Hope Hospice at Shellpoint, and to our Pennsylvania team, Stacia Bradley, Lucy Martinez-Zuviria, Dr. Jane Ferry, Dr. Tom Peacock, Home Instead and the hospice team at Grandview Hospital. I offer a prayer of gratitude to my dear friend, Rev. Tim Lannon, SJ, who kindly gave both Mom and Dad their spiritual farewell.

I offer my lifelong love to my wonderful brother, Jack, and his family, Sandy, Kelley and Meghan, and to my beloved husband, Joe, who was a son to my parents and who strengthened my resolve to write this story. (And a pat on the head to my writing companion, Rocky, who warms my feet and my heart.)

Most of all, I thank God for the blessing of Mary and Ray Finlayson. I know that I am a lucky woman to have been born their daughter.

about the author

Mary Lou Quinlan has written inspirational features for *Real Simple*; *O, The Oprah Magazine*; *More* and other magazines and is the author of the books *Just Ask a Woman*, *Time Off for Good Behavior* and *What She's Not Telling You*. She is the nation's leading expert on female consumer behavior, and as the founder and CEO of marketing consultancy Just Ask a Woman and of Mary Lou Quinlan & Co., she has interviewed thousands of women about their lives. Mary Lou has keynoted hundreds of conferences around the United States; has appeared on television programs such as *The CBS Early Show*, *Good Morning America*, and *Today*; and has been profiled in the *New York Times*, *The Wall Street Journal*, and *USA Today*, among many other media outlets.

Mary Lou is Jesuit-educated with an MBA from Fordham University and an honorary doctorate in communications from her alma mater, Saint Joseph's University in Philadelphia, where she earned a BA in English. She and her husband, Joe Quinlan, live in New York City and Bucks County, Pennsylvania, along with their dog, Rocky.